T0114903

ANALOG MAZES

ANALOG MAZES

Book 1

JONATHAN GRAF

Print information available on the last page.

Rev. date: 02/15/2024

To order additional copies of this book, contact:
Xlibris
844-714-8691
www.Xlibris.com
Orders@Xlibris.com
857645

For Jennifer

Directions for solving mazes

In every maze, there is one entrance and one exit. The object of the puzzle is to move from the entrance to the exit. Be careful of dead ends. If you get stumped, start at the end, and work your way to the entrance.

3

7

9

15

19

27

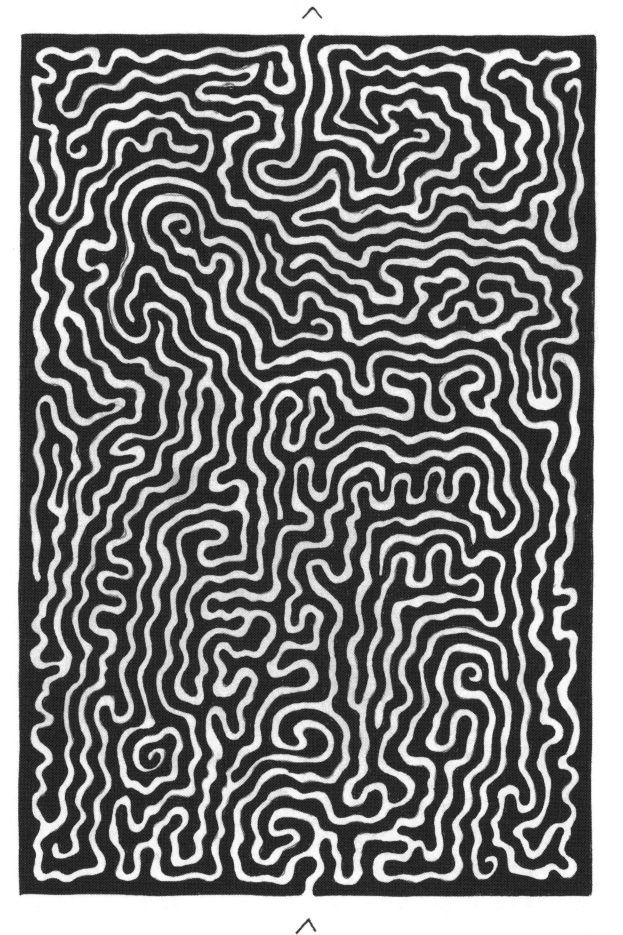

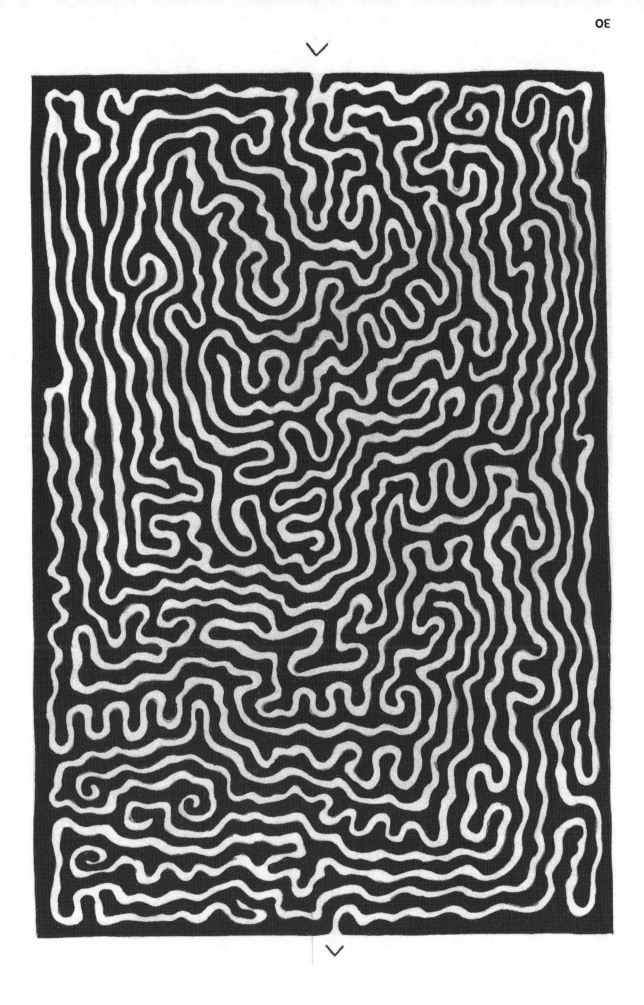

33

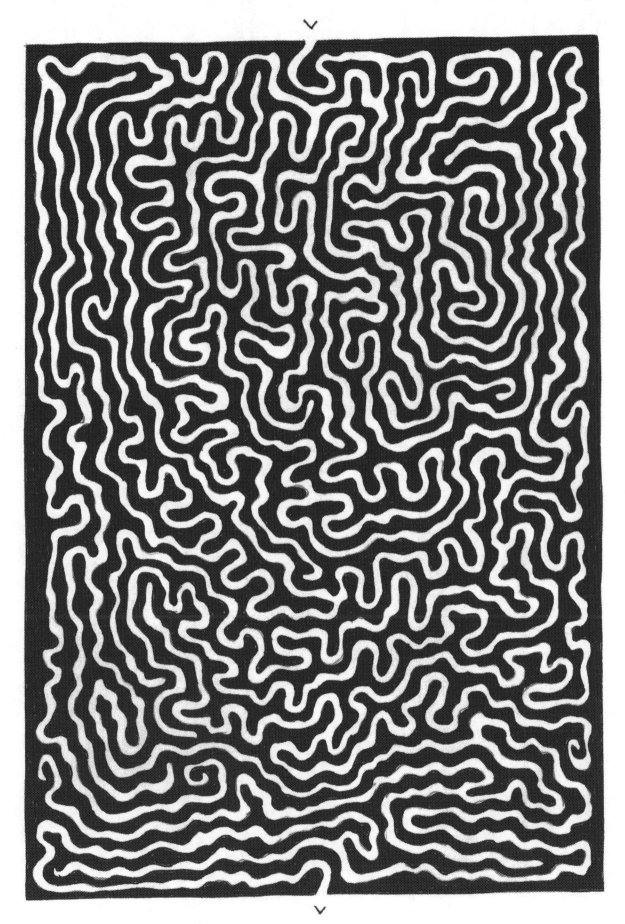

37

43

45

47

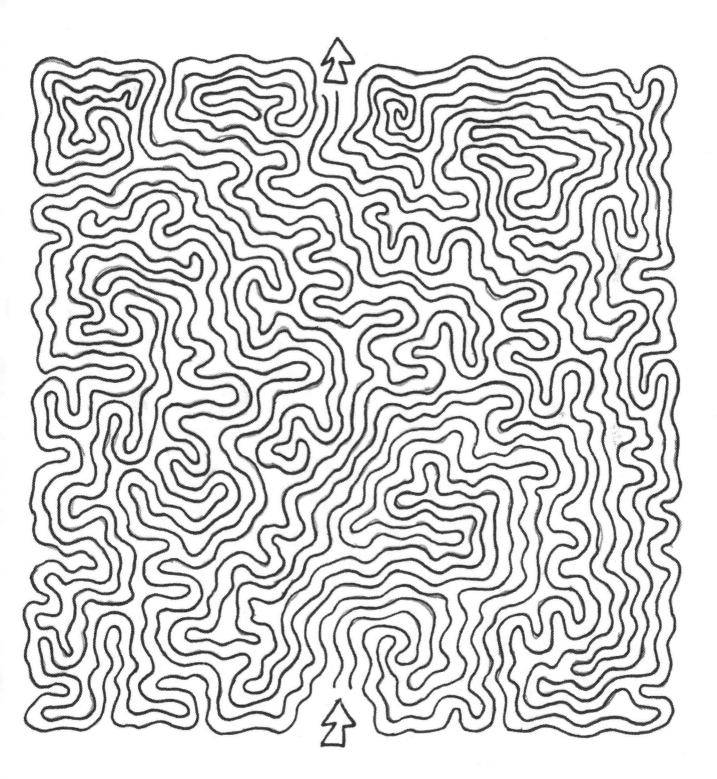

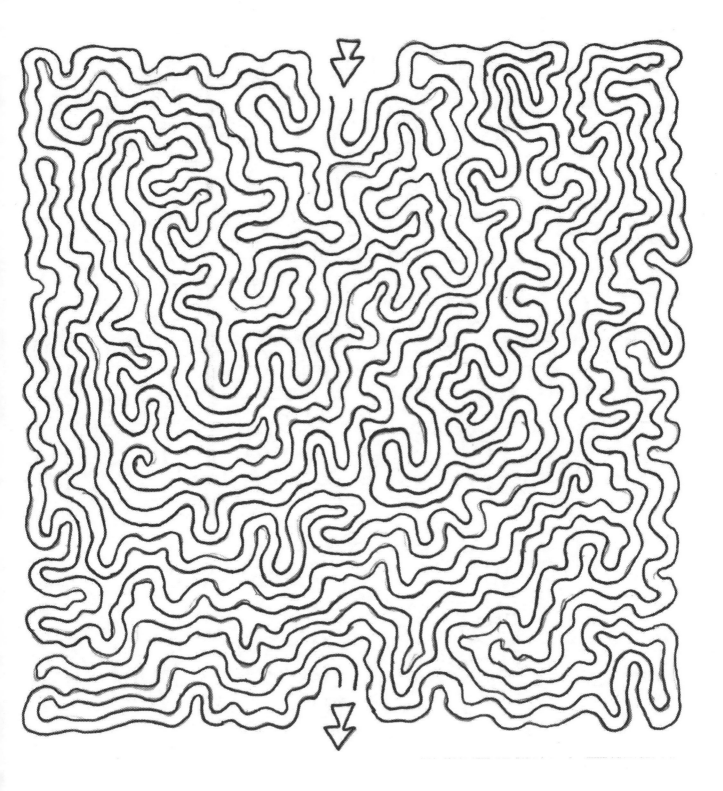

53

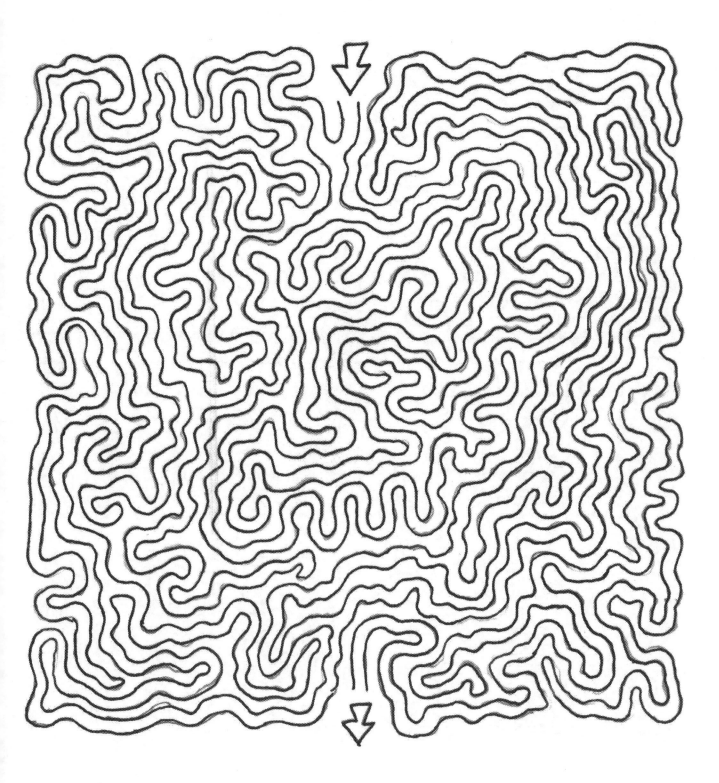

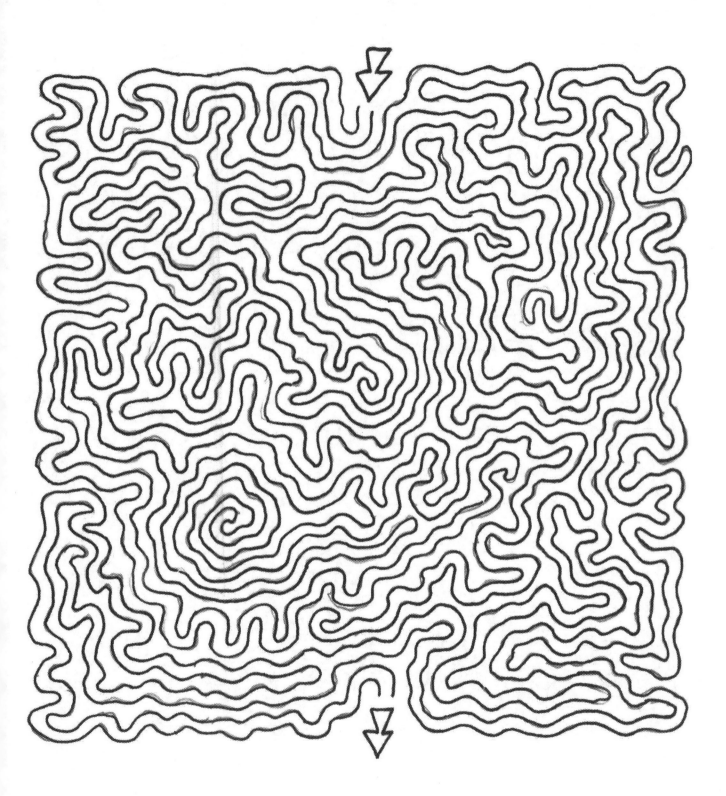

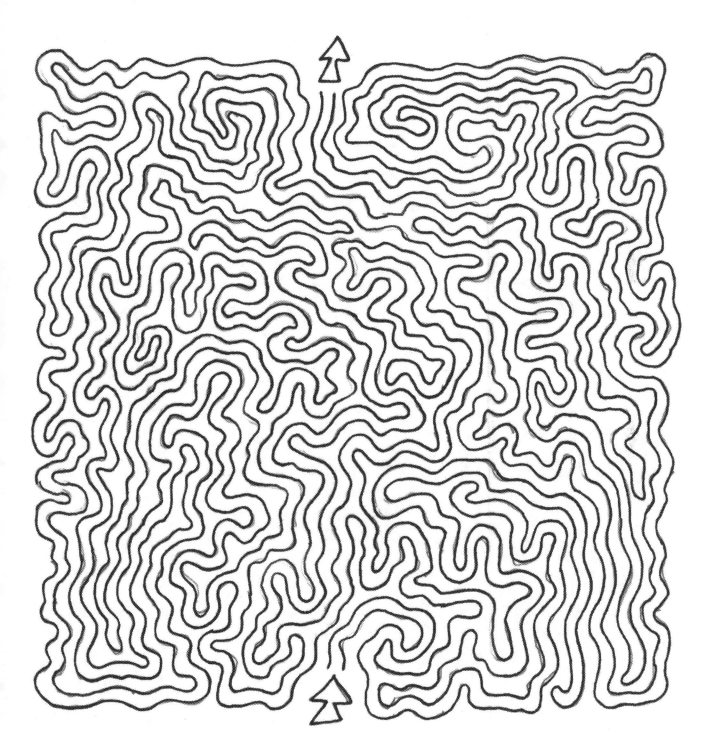

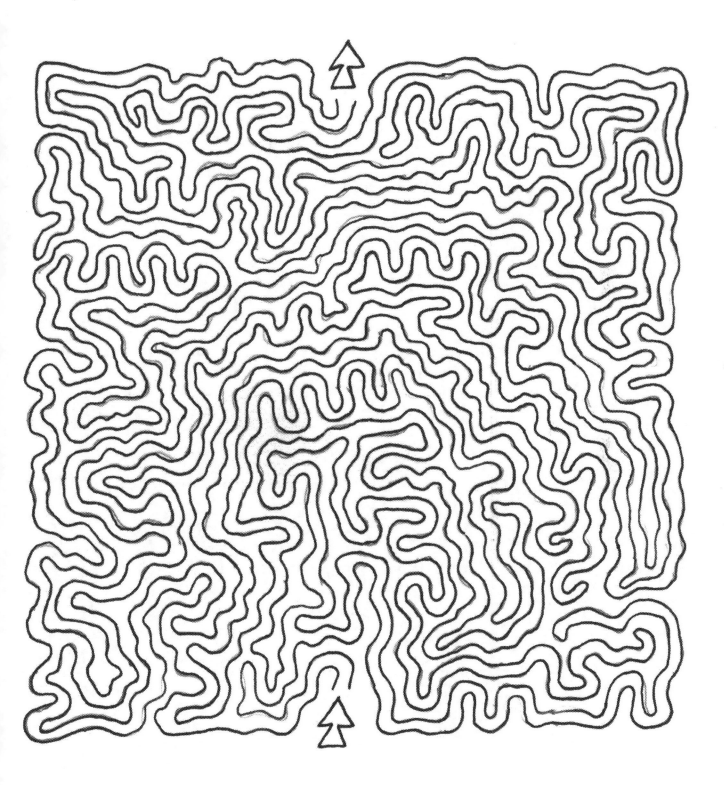

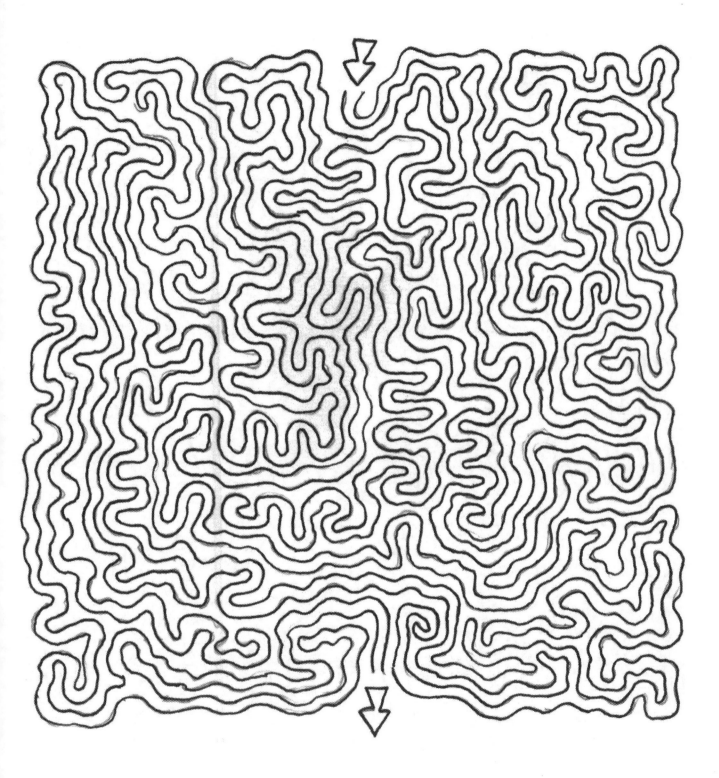

65

69

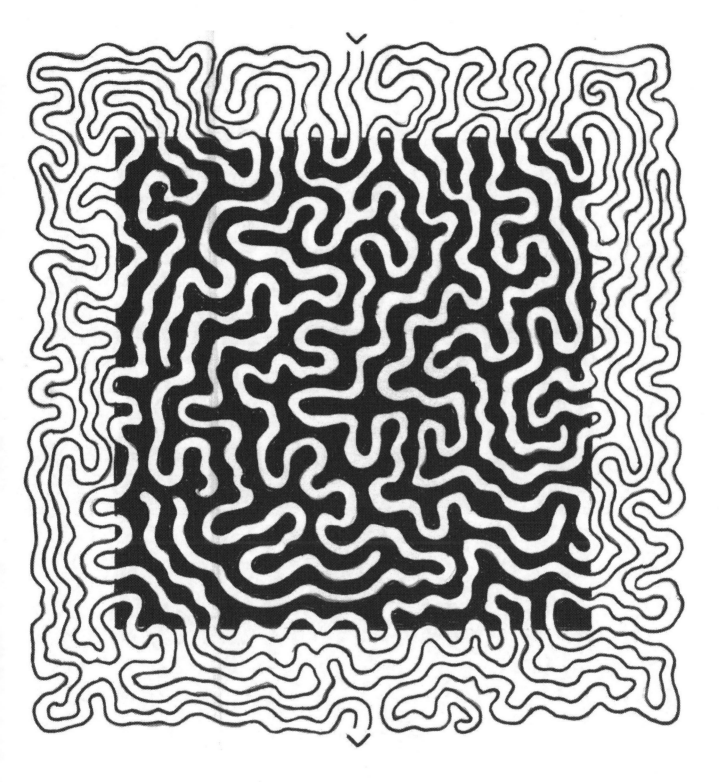

77

Printed in the United States
by Baker & Taylor Publisher Services